5-29-24

D1577721

About the author

Magdalena Lily McCarson is an artist first and foremost. She is a singer-songwriter, dancer, photographer, farmer, and believer of life. Her inspirations stem from nature, truth, and the written word. She takes great pride in embodying worldly observations, and from this, she crafts poetry and prose to encourage her readers to dream.

Magdalena lives in Peña Blanca, New Mexico, where she runs a small organic-minded community farm. She's an avid tango dancer and can be found wrapped up in someone's arms enjoying a tanda somewhere in this world.

Photography:
magdalenalilymccarson.com

Seeds Art Cafe and Farm:
seedsnewmexico.com
@seedsnewmexico on Instagram

Music:
Oxygen on Embers on Spotfiy
@oxygenonembers on Instagram

Casa Urraca Press publishes creative nonfiction, poetry, photography, and other works by authors we believe in. New Mexico and the US Southwest are rich in creative and literary talent, and the rest of the world deserves to experience our perspectives. So we champion books that belong in the conversation—books with the power, compassion, and variety to bring very different people closer together.

We are proudly centered in the high desert somewhere near Abiquiu, New Mexico. Visit us at casaurracapress.com for exquisite editions of our books and to register for workshops with our authors.

CPSIA information can be obtained
at www.ICGtesting.com
Printed in the USA
BVHW060338090322
630858BV00003B/14

9 781956 375053

"It's a daunting task to try to convey what tango is all about, yet McCarson has captured its essence in both photography and poetry. This book will envelop you with Buenos Aires' nostalgia and the magic of the embrace. Highly recommended whether you are a seasoned dancer or just hearing about tango for the first time!"

- Liz & Yannick Vanhove, international tango teachers and World Championship finalists

Tango

Other books by Magdalena Lily McCarson

Type
Wild Expectations (with Zach Hively)
The Genteel Gardener

Tango

assemblage of impossible loves

Magdalena Lily McCarson

Casa Urraca Press
ABIQUIU

Set in Ten Oldstyle and Modula OT.

25 24 23 22   1 2 3 4 5 6 7

First edition

ISBN 978-1-956375-05-3

CASA URRACA PRESS

an imprint of Casa Urraca, Ltd.
PO Box 1119
Abiquiu, New Mexico 87510
casaurracapress.com

To the dance of tango.

*May you continue to bless us all with this
journey of self-discovery and truth. I shall
continue to surrender to myself and the
beauty that you place before me,
each and every tanda.*

Contents

Tango

assemblage of impossible loves

Exposed

molinete
swarms
me

clothes
like
onions

peeling
back
layers

love
trust
try

caught
magically
stripped

Musicality

I tap

One two three four

I tap for you

I tap the backside of your shoulder
We all start at some point

Breathe

You search for the song

I tap

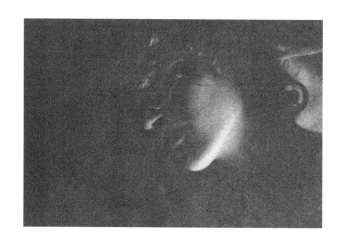

Brilliant

Strappy ribbons
Svelte leather
Colors to choose
Dresses to match

Showcased like pastries
In a sunny French window
Or diamond rings on display
At the fashionable jeweler

Cherish them
Adore them
Tango with them
Be one in them

Teach

You go

I go

We go

Free

Embrace
me

under the
jacaranda tree

Mirror my needs
allow me to be

for I am here
and I am free

Crown

Five song tanda
Orchestra prevails
Aware am I
Arrived have I

Embassy

braided gold chords
checkerboard floors
musical veil adds more
shed it all at the door

Thinking

Glorious Glorieta
stars sparkling
faces smiling

Petals of shoes
draped over edges
voluptuous crowd

In his best English
while we dance
"Stop seeenking"

Contour

vibrations and sensations
beats waft around
silence the chatter
orchestra leads

no need to perfect your follow
trust the invitation
movements speak softly
contours of melodies

pounding chests
warm hands held
circular breath shared
bodies speak quietly

Reflection

One a.m.
home.

Hot tea in hand
reminiscing the dance.

Who did you most enjoy?
Anyone move you to tears?
Someone who cared immensely?
A partner you are proud to share?

Yes, actually.
I can remember his breath.
His cadence and his care.
I drew it in.

The scent of him is still on my cheek.

Acknowledge

After ten years
you start to pass
on a few cabeceos.

But the moment you
start to cherish
the floor for
the craft and the embrace
is the exact moment you have
made a shift.
In the beginning to dance
was to dance all night.
Now I choose the Uncles,
caretakers of the dance.

The souls that move me to weep,
the ones who connect with my heart.

Chances

Where are you?
Still thinking of how you handled that work deal?

Still swallowing the upset from a relationship
twisting and turning from yesterday?

Don't worry about the kids.
They will be fine and looked after tonight.

Just be here with me.
In this vulnerable moment.

Allow me to take this chance.
Embrace me and simply dance.

Longing

Even in my dreams
you infiltrate my thoughts.

Reflections of how I felt
held in your arms.

We are strangers
but not for long.

Scanning the room
you have arrived.

Dancing and laughing
gliding together we are one.

Feelings of mutual existence and
a mountain of admiration.

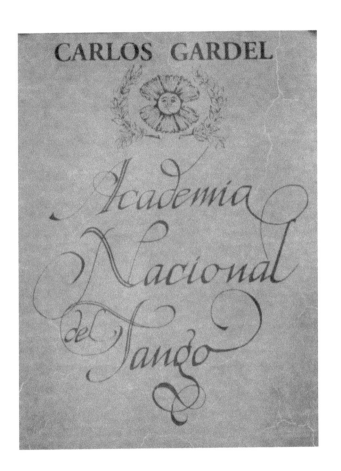

CARLOS GARDEL

Academia Nacional del Tango

Rose

Elegantly choosing
meticulous belongings
shining light upon
the brightest sight.

From across the room
reflections in the mirror
taking a step to see
what makes me.

Simple but methodical
opportunities to find
moments to take in
a joyous smile.

A genteel flower
smelling of softness
color of strength
beauty and grace.

Withstanding
the heat
of
the night.

Makers

racks
rows
boxes
bows
glimmer
shine
shoes
be mine

Trust

starry	night
blind	sight
lovers'	plight
hearts	bright
burn	white
mine	tonight
travelers'	fright
newness	might
thought	quite
dancers	delight

Festivarian

Three a.m.

please

not

one

more

ocho

Speech

Holding you tonight

Shifted nuances

Distinction

Hold steady

My hands

Speak to you

My expressions

Reside here

La Luna

Reverberation
between two
heating amidst

        strangers
        feel

Meditating
honey spilled
dripping sweet

        postures
        perfect

Soothing
minds open
hearts speak

        share
        together

Amika

Warmly placed
in your embrace

One song passes
another splashes

Room heats up
your ring buttercup

Locks of red hair
a blissful air

A milonga with you
your delicate shampoo

Journeys

so far

so try

so trust

so say

so how

so can

so surrender

so long

so move

so love

so real

so much

so true

so you

Wicked

Flames encapsulate
swirling bodies
moving circulating

Building fires
building heat
shifting weight

Changing space
transporting minds
alleviating strain

Palermo

Green trees
shadowed alleys

Fig vendors
subway strangers

Art markets
friendly parties

French bulldogs
late night buses

Nightfall

Violins echo Santa Fe Drive
laughter and conversation fill
the spaces in between.

Are we up too late again
watching, observing people
post milonga advendrás?

Enrichment to the eye
beauty to the heart
fulfilling the spirit within.

Lead

Don't blame the guy

You do

YOU

Fernanda

Dancing is something created.

Based on impulse and emotion.

The form the frame the dance.

Hands, heels, belly, breath.

Present your truest self.

Pugliese

Methodical and poised
Toes spreading
Touching floor

Whirling skirts
Nude backs
Dancing forevermore

Besos

If you had been
my one and only

tanda

I'd have retired tonight
a blessed tanguera

Practica

ME:	Please don't shuffle
HIM:	I'm not shuffling
ME:	Are you present here
HIM:	What did you say
ME:	Please be aware
HIM:	Oh shit, sorry
ME:	*{lifted toenail}*

Hallways

Harlequin floor
ripples of billowing music

Cabeceos and sports coats
mustaches and cologne

A sea of Buenos Aires
dearest Salon Canning

Respite

I dream of the water
within my wrists

Flowing streets
connecting the seas

Peaceful minds brush over
tranquility calm forehead

Cordial sun upon my chest
settled kindness to share

Take it over to the pebbles
showering raining jasmine

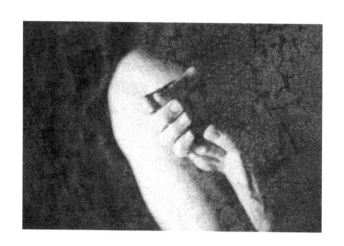

Intuition

Through your hand I know

Just how the evening will go

Release

Channel me a goodbye
one that's everlasting
                    adieu

Releasing after the tanda
exiting off the dance floor
                    floating

Energy released
forever recalling a moment
                    pleasure

Praise

The sunset moves me.
Tango moves me.

Inherently there are the stars in the sky
reflecting the glorious light in your eyes.

Holding close the beauty of all our colors.
Holding close the kindness in our hearts.

Shall we praise our shoes and the music
and take advantage of the tanda?

About the author

Magdalena Lily McCarson is an artist first and foremost. She is a singer-songwriter, dancer, photographer, farmer, and believer of life. Her inspirations stem from nature, truth, and the written word. She takes great pride in embodying worldly observations, and from this, she crafts poetry and prose to encourage her readers to dream.

Magdalena lives in Peña Blanca, New Mexico, where she runs a small organic-minded community farm. She's an avid tango dancer and can be found wrapped up in someone's arms enjoying a tanda somewhere in this world.

Photography:
magdalenalilymccarson.com

Seeds Art Cafe and Farm:
seedsnewmexico.com
@seedsnewmexico on Instagram

Music:
Oxygen on Embers on Spotfiy
@oxygenonembers on Instagram

Casa Urraca Press publishes creative nonfiction, poetry, photography, and other works by authors we believe in. New Mexico and the US Southwest are rich in creative and literary talent, and the rest of the world deserves to experience our perspectives. So we champion books that belong in the conversation—books with the power, compassion, and variety to bring very different people closer together.

We are proudly centered in the high desert somewhere near Abiquiu, New Mexico. Visit us at casaurracapress.com for exquisite editions of our books and to register for workshops with our authors.

CPSIA information can be obtained
at www.ICGtesting.com
Printed in the USA
BVHW060338090322
630858BV00003B/14